EQUIZ
Intermediate

British Library Cataloguing in Publication Data
A catalogue record for this book is available from the British Library

ISBN 0.85131.654.9

Published in Great Britain in 1996 by
J. A. Allen and Company Limited,
1 Lower Grosvenor Place,
Buckingham Palace Road,
London, SW1W OEL.

Typeset in Great Britain by Textype Typesetters, Cambridge.
Printed in Great Britain by Hillman Printers (Frome) Ltd, Somerset.

EQUIZ
Intermediate

VANESSA BRITTON

J. A. Allen
London

PART 1

Horse management

Anatomy and physiology

1 How many pairs of ribs does a horse normally have?
a) 18 ☐ **b)** 8 ☐ **c)** 24 ☐

2 Join up the sentences concerning the age at which a young horse cuts various types of teeth.

a) Adult central incisors are cut between

i) 4½ and 5 years of age.

b) Adult corner incisors are cut between

ii) 2½ and 3 years of age.

c) Adult lateral incisors are cut between

iii) 3½ and 4 years of age.

3 What *B* is the mechanics of movement? B_____

4
a) Generally speaking, there are two distinct parts to a horse's skeleton. Can you name them?
1 _____ **2** _____

b) Give three reasons why we need to know about the horse's skeleton and, in particular, where the bones are located.

1) _____

2) _____

3) _____

5 The diagram shows one of the distinct parts given in **4a)**.

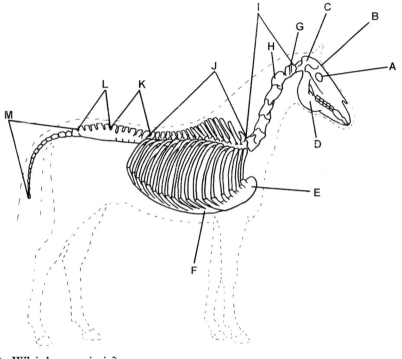

a) Which part is it? _____

b) Fill in the labels:

A _____ B _____ C _____ D _____

E _____ F _____ G _____ H _____

I _____ J _____ K _____ L _____

M _____

6 Bones are covered with a tough, thin membrane known as the periosteum.   true ☐   false ☐

7 Consider these statements about tendons.

a) They are cords which attach muscles to bone.
true ☐   false ☐

b) They consist of a fibrous tissue called callogon.
true ☐   false ☐

c) The reason they do not heal quickly if damaged is because they have a poor blood supply.   true ☐   false ☐

d) They are far more elastic than muscles, so prevent many muscle injuries.   true ☐   false ☐

8 The horse's skin consists of an inner and outer layer. What are these two layers called?

a) The inner layer is called the: _____

b) The outer layer is called the: _____

9 What *C* covers the ends of bones to prevent friction in the joints? C_____

10 The diagram shows the second part of the horse's skeleton.

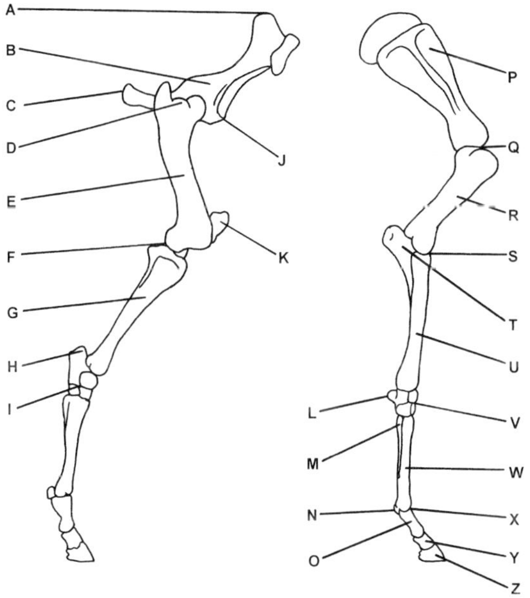

a) Which part is it? _____

b) Fill in the labels:

A _____ B _____ C _____ D _____

E _____ F _____ G _____ H _____

I _____ J _____ K _____ L _____

M _____ N _____ O _____ P _____

Q _____ R _____ S _____ T _____

U _____ V _____ W _____ X _____

Y _____ Z _____

Psychology

11 What is the combination of brain and spinal cord known as?

_____

12 Do all actions have to come from the brain in the first instance?

a) No, reflex actions are carried out without going through the brain first. ☐

b) Yes, it is impossible for the horse to do anything without a message coming first from the brain. ☐

c) The only action that does not come from the brain is the beating of the heart. ☐

13 Join up the sentences.

a) Reflex action is   **i**) that which is consciously controlled by the horse.

b) Automatic action is **ii**) that which is not consciously controlled by the horse.

c) Voluntary action is **iii**) an immediate action to stimuli without conscious thought.

14 Horses are gregarious animals. What does this mean?

_____

_____

15 This diagram represents the horse's sensory systems. In order to understand horses we should learn a little about their senses and how these affect our actions towards them. Each of the letters represents a sense or components of the sensory system. Fill in the labels:

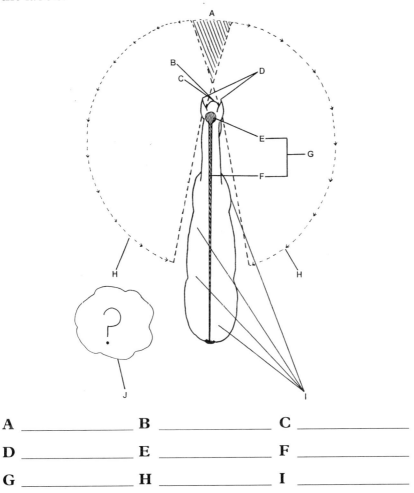

A _____ **B** _____ **C** _____

D _____ **E** _____ **F** _____

G _____ **H** _____ **I** _____

J _____

16 What two basic instincts govern all horses?

a) _____

b) _____

17 The reason why horses usually sleep standing up is the same reason why they eat almost continually without allowing their stomachs to become full. What is this reason?

a) To ensure maximum weight gain with the minimum of effort ☐

b) To enable them to take flight immediately without restriction. ☐

c) To ensure that their systems are sufficiently satisfied without over-indulgence. ☐

18 To minimise the development of stable vices the horse should be provided with constant distractions, such as a busy yard and music.   true ☐   false ☐

19 Join up the sentences.

a) A stallion's stable should be

      i) between two dominant horses.

b) The stable of a timid horse should not be

      ii) where all activity can be observed.

c) The stable of a horse with little confidence should be

      iii) in a peaceful corner of the yard.

20 By taking into account the horse's natural lifestyle most problems can be comprehended and solved. In this diagram we can see someone dealing with a biting horse by allowing it to bite the metal curry comb, instead of them! Is this a good idea? (Give the reasons for your answer.)

_____

_____

_____

Horse health

21 Finish the sentence. 'A good definition of a "well-covered" horse would be:

_____

_____

22 What colours should the following be?

a) Mucous membranes   _____

b) Normal urine   _____

c) Normal droppings   _____

23 How should you perform a capillary refill test?

a) By pressing on the gum to restrict blood flow.   ☐

b) By pinching a fold of skin on the neck.   ☐

c) By taking a blood sample from the jugular vein.   ☐

11

24 What *A* may be indicated by pale mucous membranes?

A _____

25 Study the diagram, then answer the following questions.

a) What does the diagram represent?

_____

_____

b) How is poor digestion and a loss of condition related to diagram A?

_____

_____

c) How often should the process from A to B be attended to?

_____

_____

d) Why does A occur at all?

_____

_____

26 When energy levels required for immediate exercise are exhausted, fatigue may occur. What three things need to be provided in order to reverse the situation?

a) _____

b) _____

c) _____

27 Which is the cause of upper respiratory diseases and abortion in mares?

a) Equine herpes virus 1 ☐

b) Equine herpes virus 4 ☐

c) Equine herpes virus 3 ☐

28 Link up the words to give the veterinary and common names of worms.

a) Red worm i) *Gastrophilus*

b) Pinworm ii) *Dictyocaulus*

c) White round worm iii) *Oxyuris*

d) Lungworm iv) *Parascaris*

e) Bots v) *Strongylus*

29 What *I* is a stoppage or blockage of part of the alimentary tract? I_____

30 What is the name of this test and what is its purpose?

_____

_____

Common ailments

31 Fill in the missing words.

B_____ is nearly always accompanied by s_____ and h_____.
Where this is on the l____ area you can reduce it by c____ h_____.
Increase the p_____ once the horse is used to the feel.

32 During a lecture you are asked to list six points that are most important in the nursing of sick horses. What answers do you give?

1 _____
2 _____
3 _____
4 _____
5 _____
6 _____

33 There are three main causes/types of cough. Can you name them?

1 _____ 2 _____ 3 _____

34 Epistaxis is the name used to describe a nosebleed which may occur after work or during rest.   true ☐   false ☐

35 Which shows the correct way to put on a hock bandage?

A ☐   **B** ☐   **C** ☐

36 What *R* is a highly contagious skin disease that is caused by a fungus, and also affects humans. R_____

37 There are two more common names for urticaria.

a) Can you name one of them? _____

b) Describe it?

_____

38 Splints are bodies of new bone which form at the junction between the splint and the cannon bone on the inside of the forelegs. What name is given to this new bone formation?

a) Exostosis. ☐

b) Splintosis. ☐

c) Fixosis. ☐

39 Describe 'nail-bind'.

_____

_____

40 This is a picture of a sucking louse. Can such a louse be seen with the naked eye.   yes ☐   no ☐

General management

41 Why do most field gates open inwards into the field?

a) To stop other horses from barging out while you are taking one horse out of the field. ☐

b) To prevent them from being blown open during windy weather when trying to lead a horse out of the field. ☐

c) To prevent horses from opening them themselves. ☐

42 Is it a good idea to take feed in a bucket into the field when catching a horse?

Give the reasons for your answer: _____
_____

43 How long would it take an experienced person to muck out a stable properly?

a) 10–15 minutes ☐

b) 15–20 minutes ☐

c) Half an hour ☐

44 Which is considered the best way of handling horses?

a) You should try to achieve your aims by reward. ☐

b) You should try to achieve your aims by punishment. ☐

c) You should try to reason with the horse. ☐

45 Name all the items of a well-stocked grooming kit:

A _____ B _____ C _____ D _____

E _____ F _____ G _____ H _____

I _____ J _____ K _____ L _____

M _____ N _____ O _____

46 Explain why horses are naturally nervous of dark or shady areas.

_____

_____

_____

47 Is it acceptable to slap a horse on the nose immediately it bites you?

_____

48 When going into the stable, you should discourage the horse from coming to the door to greet you.   true ☐   false ☐

49 Is it advisable to keep a bridle on a young horse when turning it out? Give the reasons for your answer.

_____

_____

_____

50 On the diagram mark the horse's most sensitive areas.

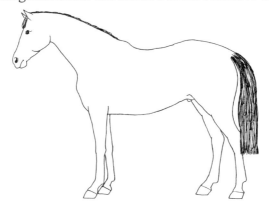

The horse at grass

51 How high should the bottom rail of post and rail fencing be from the ground?

a) 45 cm (18 in). ☐

b) 25 cm (10 in). ☐

c) 65 cm (26 in). ☐

52 Give reasons why (a) it should be no higher and (b) no lower.

a) _____

b) _____

53 Are buttercups poisonous to horses?   yes ☐   no ☐

54 Hedgerows are often the best type of enclosure as horses cannot get through them nor hurt themselves on them. Would a hedgerow made up of privet, laurel and rhododendron be a good choice for horses? Why?

_____

_____

_____

55 This water trough is serving adjoining fields. Given its purpose, is it a good or a poor design?

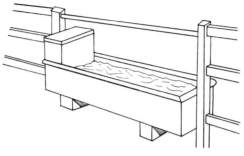

_____

_____

56 What _L_ are the areas horses like best and so graze very short?

L_____

57 Name three methods of reducing the worm burden of a regularly grazed paddock.

1 _____

2 _____

3 _____

58 How would you secure a gate against thieves?

a) By turning the top hinge downwards and padlocking both ends with a strong chain. ☐

b) By making sure the top hinge faces upwards and putting an alarm on the gate. ☐

c) By electrifying the gate. ☐

59 Plants like nettles and thistles are not poisonous to the horse but should still be removed from the paddock. Why is this?

_____

_____

60 This fencing is known as rail and diamond mesh. Which of the following statements describing it are true?

a) It is extremely safe for horses and requires minimal maintenance.   true ☐   false ☐

b) It is very expensive but the small holes prevent a horse putting his feet through the wire.   true ☐   false ☐

c) It is cheap and not suitable for horses as they can get their feet through it.   true ☐   false ☐

d) It requires a great deal of maintenance but is, nevertheless, initially cheap to buy.   true ☐   false ☐

Feeding

61 What are the seven nutrients required for health and fitness?

1 _____   2 _____   3 _____

4 _____   5 _____   6 _____

7 _____

62 Join up the sentences.

a) Proteins are required for   **i)** heat, energy and warmth.

b) Fats are needed for   **ii)** growth and repair.

c) Carbohydrate is need for   **iii)** heat and energy.

63 It is very important to feed a balanced diet. What are the normal proportions of such a diet?

20

a) One-sixth fat, one-sixth protein and two-thirds carbohydrate. ☐

b) One-sixth fat, one-sixth carbohydrate, two-thirds protein. ☐

c) One-third fat, one-third protein, one-third carbohydrate. ☐

64 What *M* is a byproduct of sugar that is fed in small quantities to supply energy and possibly to tempt a fussy feeder? M_____

65 The diagram shows a section through a grain commonly fed to horses.

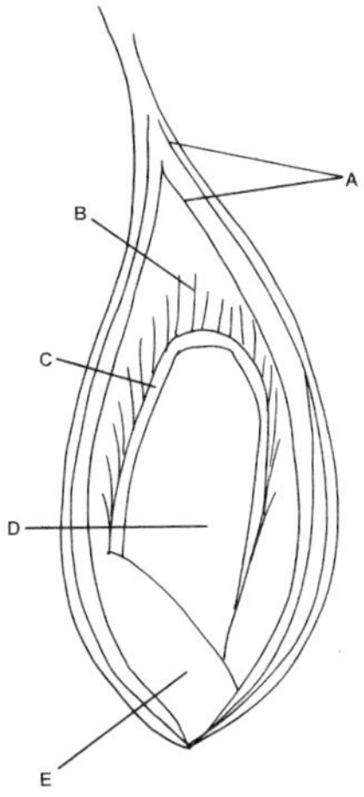

a) What is the grain?

_____   _____

b) Fill in the labels.

A _____ B _____ C _____

D _____ E _____

66 Oats are the best feed for horses. Explain why this is so and name any disadvantages they may have.

_____

_____

67 Peas and beans are non-heating foods so they can be fed in large quantities to ponies as a cheap food source. true ☐ false ☐

68 What is the maximum weight of hard feed that should be given at any one meal?

a) 900 g (2 lb). ☐

b) 1.4 kg (3 lb). ☐

c) 1.8 kg (4 lb). ☐

69 You are aware that your horse has a calcium deficiency. What do you add to the feed to counteract this?

a) Limestone flour. ☐

b) Sodium carbonate. ☐

c) Cornflour. ☐

70a) On the diagram mark what two measurements you would take to get an approximate body weight in pounds.

b) How would you then calculate the weight?

_____

c) How would you convert the weight in pounds to kilograms?

_____

How the horse works

71 Between what ages is the horse's digestive system most efficient?

a) 1–5 years. ☐

b) 8–12 years. ☐

c) 12–16 years. ☐

72 What *A* is the complete digestive tract from lips to anus?
A_____

73 Explain why lack of exercise can contribute to defective limb circulation which may result in filled legs.

_____
_____
_____

74 The circulatory system consists of the heart and all blood vessels. true ☐ or false ☐

75 This diagram represents the upper respiratory and digestive passages of the horse. Can you fill in the labels?

A _____ **B** _____ **C** _____

D _____ **E** _____ **F** _____

G _____

76 What role does the epiglottis play in the digestive system?

a) It prevents the horse from being able to vomit. ☐

b) It prevents food from passing down the trachea. ☐

c) It enables water to flow in and out of the stomach. ☐

77 Name four primary functions of the skin:

1 _____   2 _____

3 _____   4 _____

78 Join up the sentences:

a) Motor nerves   **i)** register sensation.

b) Autonomic nerves   **ii)** regulate movement.

c) Sensory nerves   **iii)** control automatic functions and responses.

79 What *D* is a most important function performed by the liver?
D _____

80 In order to understand what may go wrong with the eye, it helps to have an understanding of its structure. Here is a cross-section of a horse's eye. Can you fill in the labels?

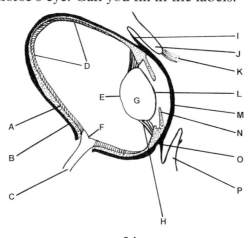

A _____ B _____ C _____

D _____ E _____ F _____

G _____ H _____ I _____

J _____ K _____ L _____

M _____ N _____ O _____

P _____

Saddlery and clothing

81 What are the five bit families?

1 _____ 2 _____ 3 _____

4 _____ 5 _____

82 Where would you find a point pocket?

a) Underneath the saddle flap, next to the girth webbing. ☐

b) On an American bridle. ☐

c) On the saddle of a driving harness. ☐

83 In how many widths are saddle trees normally made?

_____

84 What are the seven control points influenced by the use of various bridles and bits?

1 _____ 2 _____

3 _____ 4 _____

5 _____ 6 _____

7 _____

85 What is this type of bridling/biting system called?

---

86 By how much should a saddle pommel clear the withers, without a rider on top?

a) 4 cm (1½ in). ☐

b) 7 cm (2¾ in). ☐

c) 10 cm (4 in). ☐

87 Cross out the wrong words to make the sentences correct:

Bits, such as *curbs/gags*, which have shanks exert pressure on the *poll/bars of the mouth* by leverage. The *longer/shorter* the shank above the mouthpiece the more leverage there is on the *poll/bars of the mouth*. However, the *shorter/longer* the shank below the mouthpiece, the more leverage there is on the *poll/bars*.

88 What *J* are lumps of grease on tack? J_____.

89 The type of sweat rug that looks like a string vest serves no purpose unless used with an insulating layer over the top.
true ☐   false ☐

90 Name the parts of a saddle.

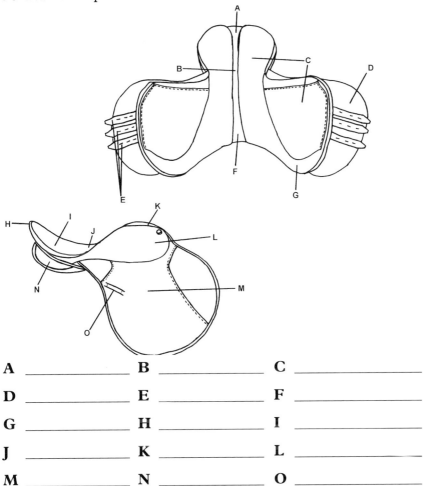

A _____	**B** _____	**C** _____
D _____	**E** _____	**F** _____
G _____	**H** _____	**I** _____
J _____	**K** _____	**L** _____
M _____	**N** _____	**O** _____

The foot and shoeing

91 Give four reasons why the horse's foot is designed as it is.

1 _____ 2 _____

3 _____ 4 _____

92 What *P* is a thin layer of skin that grows down over the hoof wall from just above the coronet. P_____

93 Fill in the missing words: 'The w_____ l_____ is the visible part of the h_____ l_____ and can be seen between the edge of the sole and the wall.

94 What bone is nearest to the toe of the foot?

a) Pedal bone. ☐

b) Navicular bone. ☐

c) Short pastern. ☐

95 In order to understand the shoeing process and to help to locate possible sites of injury, it is important to learn about the external and internal structures of a horse's foot. Fill in the labels.

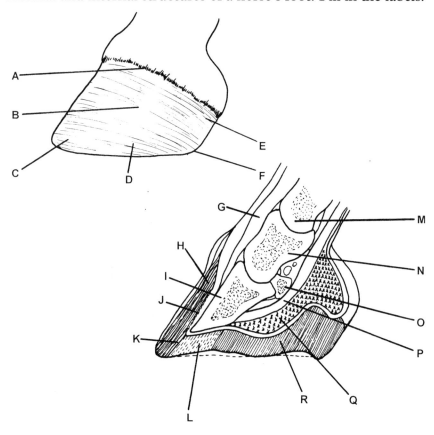

A _____ B _____ C _____ D_____

E _____ F _____ G _____ H_____

I _____ J _____ K _____ L_____

M _____ N _____ O _____ P_____

Q _____ R _____

96 What three tools does the farrier need in order to remove an old shoe?

1 _____ 2 _____ 3 _____

97 What is a 'fuller'?

a) It is the clip which helps to keep the shoe in place, or prevent it from slipping. ☐

b) It is the ground-bearing surface. ☐

c) It is the groove in which the nails sit. ☐

98 Why is it unwise to exercise a newly shod horse at fast gaits?

_____

99 What *C* separates the hoof wall from the lower limb?

C _____

100 What is the normal foot/pastern angle in (a) the hind limb and (b) the fore limb, represented by the arrowed angles on the diagram?

A _____   B _____

PART 2

Equitation and teaching

Gaits and action

101 What subdivisions are generally recognised within walk, trot and canter gaits?

a) _____

b) _____

102 What _F_ is the horse's outline and posture often described as?
F_____

103 Lateral and longitudinal are two words often used when schooling horses. Describe what they mean.

Lateral means: _____

Longitudinal means: _____

104 What is being described? This is where the horse carries his balance mostly over his front legs. His head and neck are lowered and extended and his hind legs, which may lack engagement, push, rather than carry the weight.

_____

_____

105 What is wrong here?

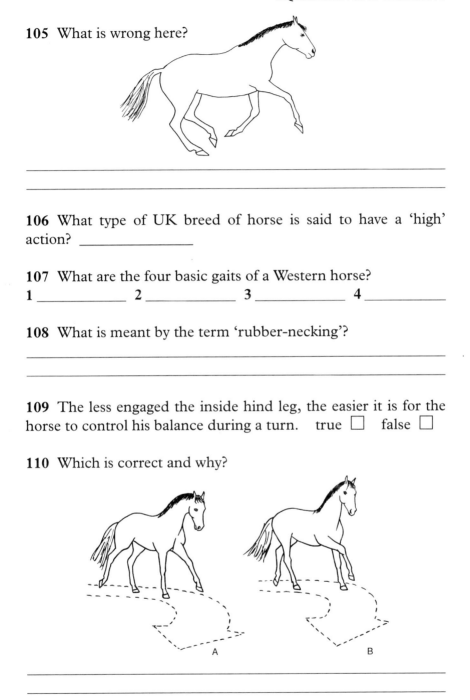

_____

_____

106 What type of UK breed of horse is said to have a 'high' action? _____

107 What are the four basic gaits of a Western horse?
1 _____ 2 _____ 3 _____ 4 _____

108 What is meant by the term 'rubber-necking'?

_____

_____

109 The less engaged the inside hind leg, the easier it is for the horse to control his balance during a turn.   true ☐   false ☐

110 Which is correct and why?

_____

_____

School work

111 What *L* movements are leg-yielding, shoulder-in, travers, renvers and half-pass termed as? L_____

112 What is this movement? The horse moves forwards and sideways; is slightly bent away from the direction of the movement, but his body is parallel to the track. The inside legs cross over in front of the outside legs.

a) Leg yielding. ☐

b) Shoulder-in. ☐

c) Half-pass. ☐

113 Join up the sentences.

a) Travers is   **i)** when the head is to the wall.

b) Renvers is   **ii)** ridden on the diagonal in the school.

c) Half-pass is   **iii)** when the quarters are to the wall.

114 What movement/position is it useful to adopt before asking for counter-canter?

a) Shoulder-in. ☐

b) Travers. ☐

c) Half-pass. ☐

115 What movement does this diagram represent and what does it help to develop?

_____

_____

116 What is the difference between lateral and vertical flexion?

_____

117 Rein-back is, technically, a movement in two-time.
true ☐   false ☐

118 Cross out the wrong words to make the sentences correct.

Shoulder-in/half-pass is ridden on _three/four_ tracks, at an angle of _45/30_ degrees to the wall or centre line. The horse is bent _towards/away from_ the direction in which he is moving.

119 Why, when schooling horses, are we always working towards getting the horse to transfer his weight on to his hind quarters?

_____

_____

120 Study this diagram and then answer the following questions:

a) Comment on the horse's way of going. _____

_____

_____

b) Name three reasons why this may have happened.
1 _____
2 _____
3 _____

Fitness and exercise

121 Why is walking exercise so important at the start of a fitness programme?

_____

_____

122 What is the best way to increase fitness without increasing concussion on the limbs?

a) To do uphill work.   ☐

b) To do galloping work on grass.   ☐

c) To do faster road work.   ☐

123 What _R_ should you observe throughout a horse's fitness training programme in order to ensure that you are not doing too much work too soon? R_____

124 The more common type of horse will get fit quicker than a better-bred horse.   true ☐   false ☐

125 Take a look at the diagram. Figure A shows the passage of airflow while the horse's head is in a normal position during exercise. Figure B shows a fixed head position during exercise. Comment on the consequences of B.

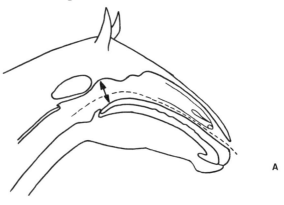

A

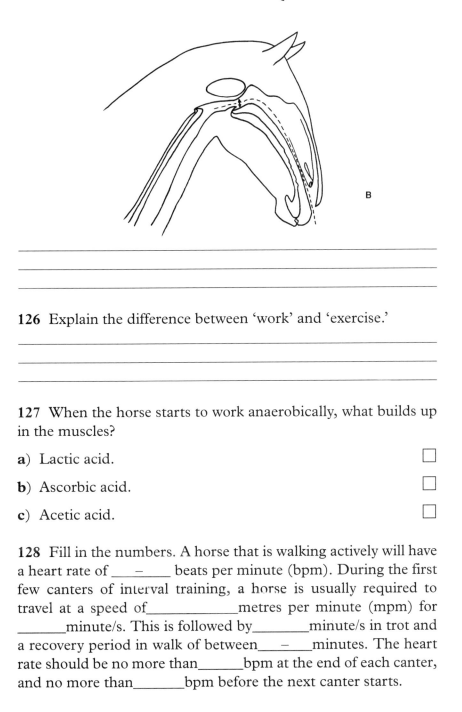

B

_____

_____

_____

126 Explain the difference between 'work' and 'exercise.'

_____

_____

_____

127 When the horse starts to work anaerobically, what builds up in the muscles?

a) Lactic acid. ☐

b) Ascorbic acid. ☐

c) Acetic acid. ☐

128 Fill in the numbers. A horse that is walking actively will have a heart rate of ____–____ beats per minute (bpm). During the first few canters of interval training, a horse is usually required to travel at a speed of_____metres per minute (mpm) for _____minute/s. This is followed by_____minute/s in trot and a recovery period in walk of between____–____minutes. The heart rate should be no more than_____bpm at the end of each canter, and no more than_____bpm before the next canter starts.

129 If a horse were travelling 400 metres in one minute (400 mpm) in what gait would he be travelling?

a) A steady trot. ☐

b) A brisk canter. ☐

c) A fast gallop. ☐

130a) On the diagram, draw a circle to represent the location of the horse's centre of gravity.

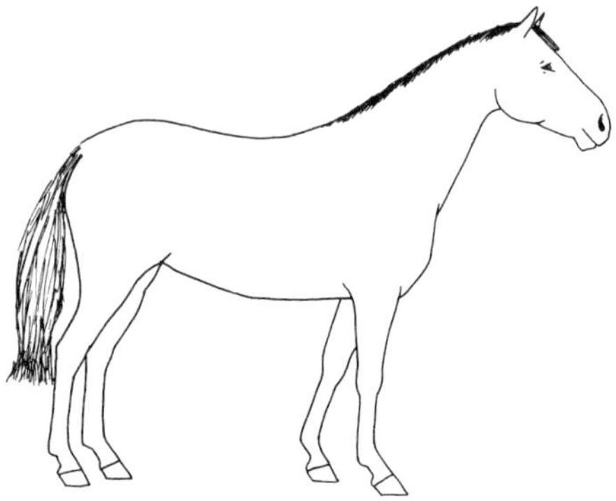

b) Describe how the position will change if the horse's head is lifted, or lowered?

_____

_____

Gymnastic development

131 Jumping is improved by any gymnastic work which improves the canter stride.   true ☐   false ☐

132 If a horse starts to rush the poles during gymnastic training, what should you do?

a) Circle him away and rebalance and relax him before coming again. ☐

b) Do a series of half-halts, but under no circumstances turn him away. ☐

c) Drop the reins and allow him to knock the poles so that he will not do it again. ☐

133 When lungeing a horse over poles or grids, what should he wear and what should be removed?

_____

_____

134 There are six basic qualities which comprise 'gymnastic ability'. What are they?

1 _____ 2 _____ 3 _____
4 _____ 5 _____ 6 _____

135 Many horses are hampered in their movement because of a badly fitting saddle, which makes correct gymnastic development impossible. Which of these diagrams represents a well-fitting saddle, and what is the problem with the other two? Fill in your answers on page 38.

A

B

C

_____

_____

_____

_____

_____

136 If riding over trotting poles, what must the horse be allowed to do?

_____

_____

137 How many strides would a horse make between the following distances at canter?

a) Fences that are 3.5 m (11½ ft) apart will allow the horse _____ stride/s between fences.

b) Fences that are 6.5 m (21 ft) apart will allow the horse _____ stride/s between fences.

c) Fences that are 10.5 m (34 ft) apart will allow the horse _____ stride/s between fences.

138 Why are correct distances sometimes slightly altered, once the horse is performing consistently well over them?

_____

_____

139 Putting up a single fence in the centre of a figure-of-eight track can be used to teach the horse three things. What are they?

1 _____ **2** _____

3 _____

140 In what gait is this type of gymnastic work (diagram on page 39) best done, and, therefore, at what distances should these poles be set?

_____

_____

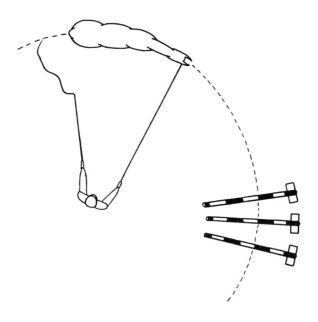

Jumping

141 Just before the moment of take-off, the horse lowers his head.   true ☐   false ☐

142 When teaching a novice rider to jump, what piece of additional equipment should be fitted to the horse?

_____

_____

143 What _P_ is a sudden slowing down in front of a fence, which may lead to a refusal if the rider has not anticipated the situation?
P_____

144 What is meant by the term 'left behind'.

_____

_____

_____

145 Take a look at the diagram.

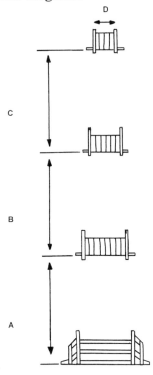

a) What is the purpose of setting out a row of fences in this manner?

_____

b) What should the distances A, B, C and D be when approaching in canter?

A: _____ **B:** _____ **C:** _____

D: _____

146 To what type of fence should a young or green horse first be introduced?

a) A cross pole. ☐

b) An upright. ☐

c) A wall. ☐

147 Name two reasons why placing poles are not used in the very early stages of training.

1 _____

2 _____

148 Why are ground lines essential?

a) Because they help the horse to assess his point of take-off. ☐

b) Because they help the horse to stand off from a fence. ☐

c) Because they help the horse to come in deep to a fence. ☐

149 Put the following in order of progressive jumping difficulty.

a) Tiger trap. ☐

b) Staircase. ☐

c) Upright. ☐

d) Square oxer. ☐

150 The two dotted lines in the diagram represent the 'take-off' zone which is the optimum area for the horse to have his hind legs placed for take-off at a fence. If line B measures 1.2 m (4 ft), what do lines A and C measure?

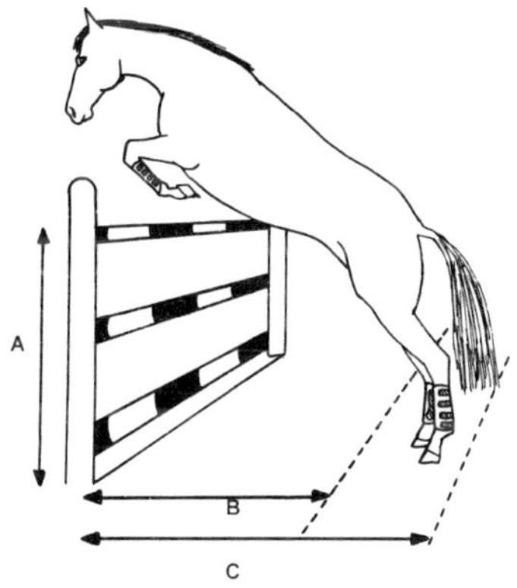

A _____ **C** _____

Cross country jumping

151 What is a coffin?

a) An obstacle that looks like a coffin resting on four corner poles. ☐

b) An obstacle with three elements, the middle one of which is a ditch. ☐

c) An obstacle at which the rider has to dismount. ☐

152 What two factors govern the severity of a bank fence?

1 _____

2 _____

153 During a cross country round it is necessary to shorten the horse's stride when approaching certain fences. Name three such fences.

1 _____ **2** _____

3 _____

154 How would you advise your pupil to jump a corner fence?

_____

_____

155 This corner fence has three possible routes. Two are marked.

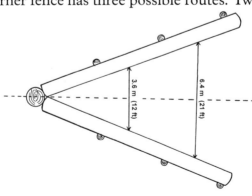

a) What is the third route?

_____

b) How many strides would the horse get in between the marked routes?

_____

156 How many penalties will a run out incur?

a) 5. ☐   **b)** 15. ☐   **c)** 20. ☐

157 When jumping cross country fences, the red flag should be on your left and the white flag on your right.   true ☐   false ☐

158 What _G_ is normally included in a timed section? G _____

159 Where the highest part of a spread fence is at the back of the obstacle, where does the horse need to take off?

a) Close to the base of the fence.   ☐

b) Further than normal away from the base.   ☐

c) In the same place as for an upright.   ☐

160 Take a look at the diagram. A and B represent possible routes. Which is the safest route and why? Fill in your answer on page 44.

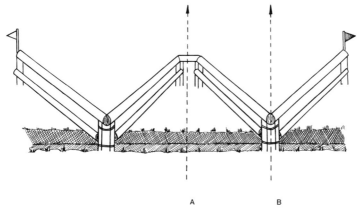

A   B

_____
_____
_____

Lungeing

161 What should be the minimum length of a lungeing rein?

a) 4 m (13 ft). ☐

b) 5 m (16½ ft). ☐

c) 6 m (19½ ft). ☐

162 There are five main reasons for lungeing a horse. What are they?

1 _____
2 _____
3 _____
4 _____
5 _____

163 What should you do with the whip when not in use?

a) Put it on the floor. ☐

b) Hold it as normal. ☐

c) Hold it backwards under your arm. ☐

164 As the horse starts to work better on the lunge, what will happen to the side reins and why?

_____
_____

165 What is this type of lungeing cavesson called and in which two ways does it differ from a normal model?

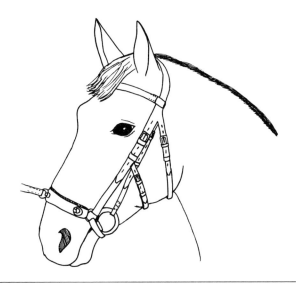

---

166 How is it best to progress to medium trot while on the lunge?

a) Drive the horse out of the circle on to a straight line for a few paces. ☐

b) Keep on the circle and speed up the pace. ☐

c) Keep on the circle, but move more yourself. ☐

167 Name the main muscle groups that are developed by lungeing?
a) _____ **b)** _____

168 What *O* might be the outcome of a horse in side reins that are too short? O_____

169 How would you deal with a horse that refuses to stop on the lunge?

a) Walk it straight into a solid wall or hedge to block its forward movement, coupled with the command 'halt'. ☐

b) Keep shortening the lunge rein until the horse cannot physically move any longer. ☐

c) Keep repeating the command 'whoa', drop the whip and then give a couple of sudden jerks on the rein. ☐

170 Is this a safe way of lungeing a youngster just beginning his training?

a) Yes, the assistant handler can soothe the horse and offer a leading hand if necessary. ☐

b) No, the assistant could be hurt, so should be standing on the outside of the horse in order to make a quick escape if necessary. ☐

c) Yes, although the assistant should be holding the horse's head with his right hand. ☐

Long-reining

171 All movements of dressage, including Grand Prix work, can be achieved by long-reining. true ☐ false ☐

172 What are the four main methods of long-reining?

1 _____ 2 _____ 3 _____ 4 _____

173 What are the 'aids' of long-reining?

1 _____ 2 _____ 3 _____ 4 _____

174 To obtain the halt, should you feel the *inside* or the *outside* rein slightly more strongly?

_____

175 What is the purpose of this manoeuvre during a long-reining session?

_____

176 A horse should never be asked to rein-back when in long reins as this only encourages rearing.   true ☐   false ☐

177 What *R* is the very first thing a horse should be conditioned to do in long reins? R_____ .

178 Although the distance does vary depending on the type of movements or exercises being performed, what is the optimum distance for the trainer to be from the horse during general schooling work on long reins?

a) 3 m (10 ft). ☐

b) 4 m (13 ft). ☐

c) 5 m (16½ ft). ☐

179 It is important to use long reins with 'feel' so that an even contact is established with the horse's own rhythm. In order to achieve this, would you take up or relax the right rein when the horse's right forefoot was *on* the ground of *off* the ground?

---

180 Comment upon the way in which this trainer is long-reining.

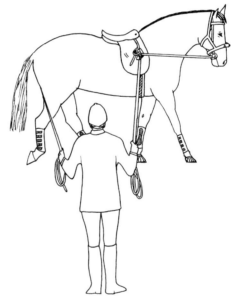

Teaching in practice

181 Join up the sentences.

a) The inside leg   **i**) controls the quarters and asks for canter.

b) The outside leg   **ii**) controls the speed and the amount of bend.

c) The inside rein   **iii**) asks for direction.

d) The outside rein   **iv**) asks the horse to go forwards and to change gait or create more impulsion within a gait.

182 During a lesson you observe the horse leaning more and more heavily on the bit, resulting in the rider being pulled forwards off her seat bones. What three things do you check?

1 _____

2 _____

3 _____

183 Fill in the missing words.
When a horse is functioning at the correct _____, with the right amount of _____ to match that _____, he will have a better chance of using his whole _____ and carrying himself forward by bringing his _____ _____ further under his _____ and using all the _____ in his _____ _____, not just his _____.

184 When you feel your pupil has achieved the right speed for their horse in trot what might you ask them to do to consolidate the lesson?

_____

_____

_____

_____

185 Being able to recognise a good position during all gaits is essential to basic training. Discuss the position of these riders performing rising trot.

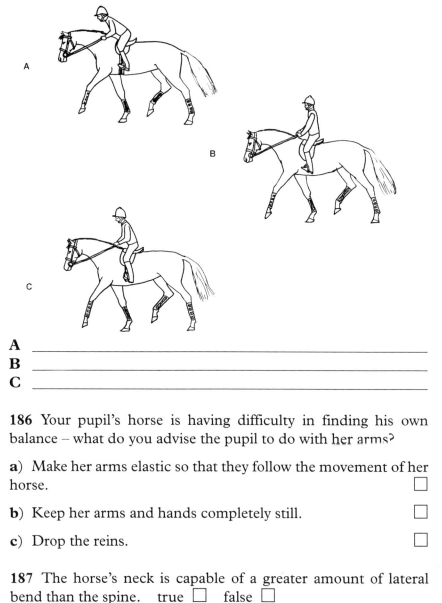

A _____

B _____

C _____

186 Your pupil's horse is having difficulty in finding his own balance – what do you advise the pupil to do with her arms?

a) Make her arms elastic so that they follow the movement of her horse. ☐

b) Keep her arms and hands completely still. ☐

c) Drop the reins. ☐

187 The horse's neck is capable of a greater amount of lateral bend than the spine.   true ☐   false ☐

188 When trying to teach a pupil the essence of suppleness, what three key words do you try to instil into them?

1 _____ **2** _____ **3** _____

189 What *I* are you asking your pupil to create by using their legs and then receiving and containing the energy with their hands.

I _____

190 This is a common lower-body exercise. Give an explanation of how you would ask a pupil to perform it.

_____

_____

_____

Riding safety and accident procedure

191 You pupil is progressing at an average rate and the horse she is riding is quiet and sensible. At what stage do you allow your pupil to venture out on a quiet hack?

a) After one private lesson. ☐

b) After six lessons in the school. ☐

c) After one year in the school. ☐

192 You wish to teach your pupil what she should do if her horse acts out of character on a ride. What do you say?

_____

_____

_____

193 You are not a good rider until you have fallen off at least seven times.   true ☐   false ☐

194 You are out on a hack with your pupil. Her horse is suddenly startled by a pheasant running out in front of him and he bolts. What have you taught her to do in such a situation?

a) Pull with all her might on both reins.　　　　　　　☐

b) Bail out.　　　　　　　　　　　　　　　　　　☐

c) Wedge one hand against the neck and try to pull the horse round in a large circle until he slows down.　　　　　☐

195 Which shows the correct line for a rider wanting to turn right at a roundabout?

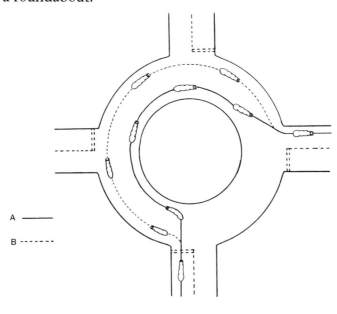

A ――――

B ‑‑‑‑‑‑‑

_____

_____

196 What sort of line across the mouth of a junction gives the signal to 'Give Way'?

_____

197 Signs which give a warning are:

a) Triangular white signs with red borders and a black picture. ☐

b) Round white signs with blue borders and a black picture. ☐

c) Triangular red signs with a white border and a blue picture. ☐

198 What does ABC stand for in relation to a riding accident?

A = _____
B = _____
C = _____

199 What test should you advise all your pupils to take once they have reached a sufficient standard?

_____

200 Are these riders riding safely?

a) Yes, they have taken up a defensive position where the motorist can see them. ☐

b) No, they should not be riding in double file. ☐

c) No, they should be trying to stop the car. ☐

Answers

Part 1   Horse management

Anatomy and physiology

1a) 18 pairs (8 of which are attached to the sternum).

2
a) + ii); **b)** + i); **c)** + iii).

3 Biomechanics.

4a) 1 The axial skeleton.   **2** The appendicular skeleton
4b)
1 In order to avoid damage to the horse during massage or grooming.
2 In order to assess if there may have been damage to a bone in relation to the site of an injury.
3 In order to assess and allow for defects in conformation.

5a) It is the axial skeleton.
5b)

A orbit	**B** cranium/skull	**C** occiput
D mandible	**E** sternum	**F** ribs
G atlas	**H** axis	**I** 7 cervical vertebrae
J 18 thoracic vertebrae	**K** 6 lumbar vertebrae	**L** 5 sacral vertebrae

M coccygeal vertebrae
(of which there may be
any number between 15
and 22)

6 True.

7a) True; **b)** false, they consist of a fibrous tissue called collagen; **c)** true; **d)** false, muscles are more elastic than tendons, so it is the tendon which more often suffers strain.

8a) The inner layer is called the the dermis; **b)** the outer layer is called the epidermis.

9 Cartilage.

10a) It is the appendicular skeleton.

b)

A tuber coxae	**B** ilium	**C** ischium
D hip joint	**E** femur	**F** stifle joint
G fibula	**H** os-calcis	**I** tarsus bones
J pubis	**K** patella	**L** pisiform
M splint bone	**N** sesamoid	**O** long pastern
P scapula	**Q** shoulder joint	**R** humerus
S elbow joint	**T** ulna	**U** radius
V carpus bones	**W** cannon bone	**X** fetlock joint
Y short pastern	**Z** pedal bone	

Psychology

11 It is known as the central nervous system.

12a) No, reflex actions are carried out without going through the brain first.

13 a) + iii); **b)** + ii); **c)** + i).

14 It means that they are sociable animals with a strong herding instinct.

15

A bifocal vision	**B** taste or smell	**C** taste or smell
D hearing	**E** brain	**F** spinal cord
G central nervous system	**H** all-round vision (sight)	
I touch	**J** sixth sense or 'feel'	

16a) Survival; **b)** reproduction.

17b) To enable them to take flight immediately without restriction.

18 False. While such an environment may interest the horse for a while, he will soon tire of it and may even find it an irritation. The best way of preventing stable vices is to try to mirror the horse's natural feeding pattern, by offering a constant supply of roughage and succulents, with concentrate feeds given little and often as appropriate. The horse should also be given adequate exercise, should be turned out for a few hours each day and should not be allowed to become lonely, stressed or bored.

19 a) + ii); **b)** + i); **c)** + iii).

20 This is a sensible course of action. Instead of the girl inflicting any sort of punishment on the horse, she is allowing him to punish himself. The horse learns by an association of ideas, so he should get the message that biting only hurts himself.

Horse health

21 '... that it has sufficient fat and muscle over its skeletal frame for no bony areas to be prominent.'

22
a) Mucous membranes – salmon-pink.
b) Normal urine – pale yellow.
c) Normal droppings – green if main diet is grass; golden if diet is hay.

23a) By pressing on the gum to restrict blood flow.

24 Anaemia.

25
a) The diagram represents (A) a horse's teeth before rasping and (B) after rasping.
b) The sharp edges will cause discomfort when eating, discouraging the horse from chewing his food properly or, in severe cases, from eating at all.
c) All horses are different but in order to prevent sharp teeth from causing problems, checks should be made approximately twice a year.
d) The horse's teeth develop sharp edges on the outer edge of the upper teeth and the inner edge of the lower teeth, due to the top jaw being wider than the bottom one. As the horse masticates, his teeth grind together and wear away, except for the overlapping edges which become pointed.

26 a) rest; **b)** food; **c)** electrolyte supplementation.

27a) Equine herpes virus 1.

28 a) + v); **b)** + iii); **c)** + iv); **d)** + ii); **e)** + i).

29 Impaction.

30 It is known as the 'flexion' or 'spavin' test and is used to diagnose spavin. The limb is flexed in this way for a period of over 30 seconds. When it is released, the horse is trotted away. If the horse has spavin he will be noticeably lame.

Common ailments

31 Bruising is nearly always accompanied by swelling and heat. Where this is on the leg area you can reduce it by cold hosing. Increase the pressure once the horse is used to the feel.

32 Any from the following list:
1 Visit frequently, causing the minimum of disturbance.
2 Check and record TPR.
3 Check if food has been eaten.
4 Monitor how frequently the horse lies down and for how long.
5 Remove droppings frequently and keep the bed dry and thick.
6 Ensure plenty of ventilation but not draughts.
7 Keep the horse warm.
8 Groom lightly, ensuring the horse stays warm. Stop at any signs of discomfort.
9 Massage warm legs to improve circulation.
10 Ensure a fresh supply of clean water is provided and monitor intake.
11 Offer tempting foods and include succulents unless the horse is having trouble eating. Remove any uneaten foods.
12 Take heed of your vet's advice.
13 Avoid bright lights if the horse has an eye injury.
14 Offer a constant supply of hay, unless otherwise directed by the vet.

33 **1** virus coughs; **2** cold coughs; **3** allergy coughs.

34 True.

35 **C** is correct as the hock joint must be left free so that the horse can still flex it when moving.

36 Ringworm.

37
a) Nettle rash or hives.
b) It is when small lumps appear and disappear without warning all over the horse's body. It may be caused by a sudden change in diet or by something the horse has eaten or reacted to.

38a) Exostosis.

39 Nail bind is caused by a shoeing nail being driven in too close to the white line. Pressure will gradually start to build up until, after a few days, lameness occurs. Removal of the nail is essential.

40 Yes.

General management

41a) To stop other horses from barging out while you are taking one horse out of the field.

42 It is not a good idea to take a bucket of feed into the field as this will attract all the horses, not just the one you want. This can lead to squabbling and you may get kicked. It also makes getting out of the field with one horse very difficult.

43b) 15–20 minutes.

44a) You should try to achieve your aims by reward. (While a system of *immediate* punishment and reward is the key to training, always look to reward where possible, rather than to punish. In this way, the horse seeks reward and in doing so learns good manners and habits, which often reduces the need to punish.)

45

A water brush	**B** body brush	**C** dandy brush
D hoof picks	**E** face and dock sponges	**F** stable rubber
G cactus cloth	**H** mane combs	**I** rubber curry comb
J plastic curry comb	**K** sweat scraper	**L** grooming/washing mitten
M metal curry comb	**N** hoof oil and brush	**O** massage/strapping pad

46 A horse's sight does not adjust quickly when coming from light into dark. Consequently, he needs a few moments to allow his sight to adjust before he can assess the situation in front of him and will therefore pause for a moment and then proceed cautiously, rather than stepping forward boldly into darkness.

47 No, never slap a horse's face or head because this can make him headshy and he may then become even more liable to bite through anxiety.

48 False. You should encourage the horse to come to the door so that you can then quickly put on the headcollar, which means you have instant control.

49 It is not advisable to have a bridle on the horse as, when you go to take it off, he may jump away from you and either bang his teeth on the bit or, worse, yank the bridle out of your hands. You are then left with a horse charging around the paddock with trailing reins and he is unlikely to want to be caught again!

50

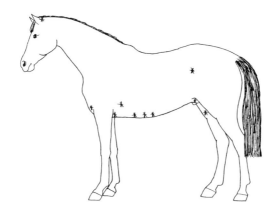

The horse at grass

51a) 45 cm (18 in).

52
a) It is low enough so that a horse or pony cannot roll underneath it, but can still graze immediately beneath it.
b) If the rail were any lower, a horse might get his foot caught over it, or jammed under it if very low.

53 Yes.

54 This would be an extremely dangerous hedge as all three plants are poisonous.

55 It is a good design as it allows easy access from either direction and the top bar prevents horses from jumping over it.

56 Lawns.

57a) harrowing; **b)** daily removal of droppings; **c)** grazing sheep or cattle on the pasture.

58a) By turning the top hinge downwards and padlocking both ends with a strong chain.

59 Such plants will compete with the grass and are likely to overtake the paddock if not removed as they can grow on poorer quality soils than grass.

60a) and **b)** are true; **c)** and **d)** are false.

Feeding

61

1 proteins   **5** vitamins
2 carbohydrates   **6** minerals
3 fats   **7** water
4 fibre

62 a) + ii); **b)** + i); **c)** + iii).

63a) One-sixth fat, one-sixth protein and two-thirds carbohydrate.

64 Molasses.

65a) It is an oat.
b)
A hull   **B** hairs
C husk   **D** endosperm
E germ

66 Oats are the best feed for horses because they contain the right values for a balanced diet (one-sixth fat, one-sixth protein and two-thirds carbohydrate). They have two disadvantages: one is that they only retain their food value for three weeks once crushed or rolled; the other is that they are known to be deficient in calcium.

67 False. They are very heating and should only be fed in small quantities and only to horses in hard work.

68c) 1.8 kg (4 lb).

69a) Limestone flour.

70a)

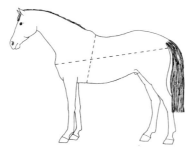

b) These measurements would then be put into the equation:
$$\frac{\text{heart girth (in)}^2 \times \text{length}}{241} = \text{bodyweight (lb)}$$
c) Multiply the pounds by 0.4536.

How the horse works

71b) 8–12 years.

72 Alimentary canal.

73 Each time a horse moves, pressure is thrust upwards from the frog between the lateral cartilages. This squeezes the blood out of the venous network and into the veins on its way back to the heart. Thus, if the horse does not receive enough exercise, circulation through the legs will be poor.

74 True.

75

A guttural pouch	**B** nasal passages
C mouth	**D** pharynx
E larynx	**F** oesophagus
G trachea	

76b) It prevents food from passing down the trachea.

77 Any from the following list:
Sensation is felt through the skin.
Heat control.
To protect internal organs and structures.
To prevent toxic agents from entering the body.
To prevent excess water loss.
To protect against irradiation.

78 a) + ii); **b)** + iii); **c)** + i).

79 Detoxification.

80

A choroid	**B** sclera	**C** optic nerve	**D** retina
E lens capsule	**F** optic disk	**G** lens	
H suspensory ligaments of lens	**I** conjuntival sac	**J** upper eyelid	
K eyelashes	**L** pupil	**M** cornea	**N** iris
O conjunctiva	**P** lower eyelid		

Saddlery and clothing

81

1 snaffle	**2** Pelham	**3** curb
4 gag	**5** bitless	

82a) Underneath the saddle flap, next to the girth webbing.

83 Three – narrow, medium and wide.

84
1 tongue
2 bars
3 corners of the mouth
4 roof of mouth
5 poll
6 nose
7 chin/curb groove

85 This is a gag bridle.

86c) 10 cm (4 in).

87 Bits, such as *curbs,* which have shanks exert pressure on the *poll* by leverage. The *longer* the shank above the mouthpiece the more leverage there is on the *poll*. However, the *longer* the shank below the mouthpiece, the more leverage there is on the *bars*.

88 Jockeys.

89 True.

90

A cantle	**B** gullet	**C** panel
D flap	**E** girth straps	**F** pommel
G knee roll	**H** cantle	**I** seat
J waist	**K** pommel	**L** skirt
M flap	**N** flocked panel	**O** keeper for stirrup leather

The foot and shoeing

91
1 To support the weight of the horse.
2 To decrease concussion.
3 To provide grip.
4 To oppose wear.

92 Periople.

93 The *white line* is the visible part of the *horny laminae* and can be seen between the edge of the sole and the wall.

94a) Pedal bone.

95

A	coronet band	**B**	wall	**C**	toe
D	quarter	**E**	periople	**F**	heel
G	common digital extensor tendon	**H**	wall	**I**	pedal bone
J	sensitive laminae	**K**	white line	**L**	sole
M	end of long pastern	**N**	short pastern bone	**O**	navicular bone
P	deep digital flexor tendon	**Q**	plantar cushion	**R**	frog

96 1 buffer; **2** pincers; **3** driving hammer.

97c) It is the groove in which the nails sit.

98 Because it takes a few days for the horn of the hoof to bed down around newly driven nails, so the shoe is less secure and in danger of being pulled off during this time.

99 Coronet.

100 a) normal angle in the hind limb is 50°; **b)** normal angle in the fore limb is 45°.

Part 2   Equitation and teaching

Gaits and action

101
a) In walk: free, medium, collected and extended subdivisions are recognised.
b) In trot and canter: working, medium, collected and extended subdivisions are recognised.

102 Frame.

103 *Lateral* means from side to side; *longitudinal* means from front to back, or back to front.

104 This describes a horse which is on his *forehand*.

105 The horse is cantering *disunited*, which means his legs are out of normal sequence.

106 A Hackney.

107

1 the walk   3 the lope

2 the jog   4 the gallop

108 This is where, when asked to turn, the horse bends his neck sideways but his body continues to move straight ahead.

109 False. It should be *more* engaged.

110 **B** is correct as this shows the correct inside canter lead (right lead on right bend). **A** is incorrect as it shows outside canter lead (left lead on right bend).

School work

111 Lateral.

112a) Leg yielding

113 **a)** + i); **b)** = iii); **c)** = ii).

114a) Shoulder-in.

115 The movement is shoulder-in which helps to develop suppleness, better collection, straightness and increased engagement of the inside hind leg as it becomes better performed.

116 Lateral flexion is where the head pivots sideways; in vertical flexion the head pivots up or down.

117 True.

118 *Shoulder-in* is ridden on *three* tracks, at an angle of *30* degrees to the wall or centre line. The horse is bent *away* from the direction in which he is moving.

119 Because this frees the shoulders and lightens the forehand, thus enabling the horse to perform more accurately.

120a) The horse is behind the bit.

b)

1 The rider may be taking too strong a contact.

2 The rider's leg and seat aids may be too weak.

3 The rider may have tried to collect the horse without having first created enough impulsion.

Fitness and exercise

121 Because it helps to tone up muscles, tendons and ligaments, making them less likely to suffer strain.

122a) To do uphill work.

123 Respiration rate.

124 False. The reverse is true.

125 While the head is in a fixed position during exercise, bridle noises may be heard. This is due to flexion in the head inhibiting airflow in the pharyngeal area, which may result in a limited volume of air reaching the lungs. The arrows show this restriction.

126 Work is done to exert the horse in order to improve fitness or education. Exercise is simply physical activity that will keep the horse healthy and maintain (but not improve) his level of fitness.

127a) Lactic acid.

128 A horse that is walking actively will have a heart rate of *60–70* bpm. During the first few canters of interval training a horse is usually required to travel at a speed of *400* mpm for *3* minutes. This is followed by *1* minute in trot and a recovery period in walk of between *3–5* minutes. The heart rate should be no more than *150* bpm at the end of each canter, and no more than *100* bpm before the next canter starts.

129b) A brisk canter.

130a)

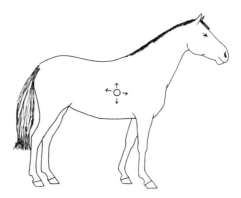

b) If the horse lifts his head, the centre of gravity will move backwards. Conversely, it will move forwards if the horse lowers his head.

Gymnastic development

131 True.

132a) Circle him away and rebalance and relax him before coming again.

133 Boots and overreach boots should be worn; the saddle, or roller and side reins should be removed.

134
1 suppleness
2 strength
3 co-ordination
4 agility
5 balance
6 rhythm

135

A is a good fit because the panels rest evenly on the muscles, the points of the tree allow freedom of movement through the shoulder blade and the gullet is clear of the spine.

B is a bad fit and a poor design. It is unbalanced backwards which will throw the rider backwards. Additionally, the panels are flat and the gullet does not clear the spine, so the saddle will create a sore back and put pressure on the spine.

C is unbalanced forwards, especially because of the unnecessary additional padding. The rider will be thrown forwards which will exacerbate the problem of the points of the tree digging into the shoulder blades.

136 He must be allowed to round his back and stretch his neck out and down. In order for him to do this well, the rider must stay slightly out of the saddle in a forward seat.

137a) Fences that are 3.5 m (11½ ft) apart will allow the horse *no* stride/s between fences. (This would be a bounce).

b) Fences that are 6.5 m (21 ft) apart will allow the horse *one* stride between fences.

c) Fences that are 10.5 m (34 ft) apart will allow the horse *two* strides between fences.

138 So that he can be taught to jump off both longer and shorter strides than normal.

139
1 To approach from either direction.
2 To approach at any angle.
3 To land on the appropriate leading leg ready for the turn to the next fence.

140 The work is best done in trot and the distance between poles for the average horse will be approximately 1.2–1.4 m (4–4½ ft) apart at the centre.

Jumping

141 True.

142 A neck strap.

143 Propping.

144 This is when the horse takes off before the rider is ready and therefore the rider does not go forward with the horse but is caught behind the movement. Unless the rider slips his/her reins the horse will then be jabbed in the mouth.

145a) A row of progressively narrower fences is useful in teaching accuracy, especially if there are no wings.
b) **A** = 6.4–7.3 m (21–24 ft); **B** = 6.4–7.3 m (21–24 ft); **C** = 6.4 m (21 ft); **D** = 1 m (3¼ ft).

146a) A cross pole.

147 1 Because they can confuse a young horse.

2 Because the horse can come to rely on them to judge his take-off, rather than assessing the fence properly.

148a) Because they help the horse to assess his point of take-off.

149 From easy to difficult: staircase, tiger trap, upright, square oxer.

150 A also measures 1.2 m (4 ft) as the take-off zone is an area between the height of the fence and 1.8 m (6ft) from the base of the fence; consequently line **C** must measure 1.8 m (6ft).

Cross country jumping

151b) An obstacle with three elements, the middle one of which is a ditch.

152
1 How sloping or vertical the sides are.
2 How much room there is on top.

153 Any from the following:
banks
water
coffins
steps up and down
bounces

154 Tell them to dissect the angle with an imaginary line and then jump at right angles to this line. Choose a fixed point somewhere beyond the fence, such as a large tree, and look towards this to help to keep their line when jumping.

155a) The third route is straight across the corner.
b) The 3.6 m (12 ft) route represents a bounce and the 6.4 m (21 ft) route represents a one-stride jump.

156c) 20.

157 False. It should be the opposite way round.

158 Gate.

159a) Close to the base of the fence so that the highest part of his jump corresponds with the highest part of the fence.

160 Route **A** is the safest route because although it requires two jumping efforts there is room for manoeuvre, while route **B** requires total accuracy for a safe jump, which means that both horse and rider must be bold and trust each other fully.

Lungeing

161c) 6 m (19½ ft).

162
To train youngsters.
To exercise horses which cannot be ridden for some reason.

To retrain horses.
To teach riders.
To undertake advanced work in-hand.

163c) Hold it backwards under your arm.

164 The side reins will become slack as the horse starts to work in a more advanced shape, i.e. shorter and rounder.

165 It is a Wels cavesson which is lighter than other designs and it is arranged so that it fastens under the bit, not above it as in the ordinary model.

166a) Drive the horse out of the circle on to a straight line for a few paces.

167a) Those of the crest of the neck;   **b)** the lumbar muscles of the back.

168 Over-bending.

169a) Walk him straight into a solid wall or hedge to block his forward movement, coupled with the command 'halt'.

170b) No, the assistant could be hurt, so should be standing on the outside of the horse in order to make a quick escape if necessary.

Long-reining

171 True.

172
1 English
2 Danish

3 French
4 Viennese

173
1 The reins
2 The voice

3 The whip
4 The trainer's position

174 The outside rein.

175 It changes the rein without having to stop.

176 False.

177 Relax!

178a) 3 m (10 ft)

179 When it was *off* the ground.

180 The rein in the right hand should not be coming through the stirrup iron. Not only will this give a backwards feel which does not encourage the horse to lengthen his stride, but, should the horse play up and run backwards, the trainer would have no control over him. In fact she would be pulling him backwards all the more!

Teaching in practice

181 a) + iv); **b)** + i); **c)** + iii); **d)** + ii)

182
1 That the rider's arms are not straight or stiff.
2 That the rider is controlling the speed correctly, and generating enough impulsion.
3 That the rider is sitting properly on her seat bones.

183 When a horse is functioning at the correct *speed*, with the right amount of *power* to match that *speed*, he will have a better chance of using his whole *body* and carrying himself forward by bringing his *hind legs* further under his *body* and using all the *joints* in his *hind legs*, not just his *hocks*.

184 Ask them to count out loud to the beat of their horse's hooves: 'one-two, one-two' all the way round the school. This will help them to achieve a constant speed and establish a good rhythm, which they can then identify during all movements and exercises.

185 Rider **A** is rising ahead of the motion and is therefore insecure. Should the horse slow or stop suddenly, she would be in danger of tumbling off over his neck.
Rider **B** is rising behind the motion. She will therefore be sitting heavily on the horse's back and may pull on the reins in order to keep her balance.
Rider **C** is rising with the motion. She therefore has a secure seat, is in balance and will require the minimum of grip to keep her seat secure. This will ensure that she is relaxed and ready for any sudden movements.

186a) Make her arms elastic so that they follow the movement of her horse.

187 True.

188 1 loose; **2** springy; **3** free (or appropriate synonyms).

189 Impulsion.

190 'Aim to sit in the middle of the saddle and feel that you are sitting equally on both seat bones. Grasp your right ankle with your right hand and bend your right leg backwards and upwards so that your heel is as close to your body as you can get it. Try to push down into your knee – think of pushing it to the ground. Be careful not to let your upper body slip sideways or tip forwards. Good – now relax.'

Riding safety and accident procedure

191b) After six lessons in the school.

192 Tell her she should push down into her heels and grip with her knees and, if the horse tries to nap or buck, push him forwards strongly. Do not tell her *not* to freeze or snatch at the reins as, if you do, she surely will!

193 False. This is absolute nonsense! You may never have fallen off but might still be a perfectly capable rider.

194c) Wedge one hand against the neck and try to pull the horse round in a large circle until he slows down. *Note*: the only time you should bail out is if the horse is running blindly into a dangerous situation, such as on to a motorway. In such an event, your life is more important than the horse's.

195 B shows the correct line – a horse and rider should always stay to the left when going round a roundabout, no matter which exit they intend to take.

196 A single unbroken white line.

197a) Triangular white signs with red borders and a black picture.

198
A = *approach* – check that you can do so safely.
B = *breathing* – check that the injured rider is breathing, give mouth to mouth resuscitation if necessary.
C = *circulation* – check to see if the rider is bleeding; if so apply pressure to the wound.
(**C** also stands for external cardiac compression – a technique which every rider should learn from an expert.)

199 The British Horse Society Riding and Road Safety Test.

200a) Yes, they have taken up a defensive position where the motorist can see them.